Brewdolph the Hop-Nosed Reindeer

ISBN-13: 978-0692044681
ISBN-10: 069204468X

Written By:

David Nelson

Illustrated by:

Chelsea Bill

www.brewdolph.com

First Edition

Manufacturing Origin and Date Available on Final Page

Dedication

To my father, Ron, for his love of craft beer that made all of this possible,
my mother, Mary Ellen, for putting up with all of the home brewing in the front yard,
and my amazing wife, Brooklyn, for encouraging *almost* all of my crazy ideas.

- David Nelson, Author

To my loving support group: James, Charles, and my family.

- Chelsea Bill, Illustrator

Special Thanks to Tyler Jones

Your creativity and suggestion that Brewdolph should be the
BrewFund company mascot inspired this story. Your energy
and passion for craft beer will always guide you to success.
Cheers!

Twas' the week before Christmas
and all through the land,

Little boys and girls
were being as bad as they can.

Parents were pushing and fighting

to get the best deal...

...all while refusing to get together

and share a meal.

"Beep! Beep! Beep!"

Went the smart phones.

"Yes sir, I can work late," the busy people moaned.

"It's one week until Christmas!"

the head Elf exclaimed

"Get to work and hurry
or I'll take the blame!"

All the Elves and Reindeer worked as hard as they could.

But poor Brewdolph wasn't doing

anything that he should.

Instead of building toys Brewdolph...

...ground his grain...

...boiled his malt...

... and cooled his wort.

But all the Elves' hard work

was coming up short.

Brewdolph was different and didn't act the same.

The others felt that it brought them

nothing but shame...

He always wore

an ugly Christmas sweater.

Because he thought it would

make him brew even better.

He dried empty bottles
on top of his head.

and all through his home
it smelled like baking bread.

His green nose
could be seen
from very
far away.

All because Brewdolph

smelled hops all day.

The craft beer cooled and
with some Christmas magic,

the beer was ready
and it was time
to let everyone have it.

"There's work to be done.

Now get out of here!"

"Yeah, Brewdolph this is no time for craft beer!"

But the workers were curious and they took a small pour...

Then they just had to have a little more.

Soon the workshop was full

of Christmas cheer!

All because of a Hop-Nosed Reindeer.

As their happiness spread,

they got back to work.

Soon the toys were built,

and the gifts were wrapped.

CRAFT BEER

CRAFT BEER

And all this happened while Brewdolph napped.

21

The Elves and Reindeer surrounded Brewdolph's house.

They tip-toed and were quiet just like a mouse.

Then they broke into a song of cheer.

About how Brewdolph saved the Holiday

with Christmas beer!

Deck the Halls

Fa-La-La-Laaa

La-La-La

Brewdolph awoke with a shock and he was uncertain.

That was, until he looked behind his window curtain.

As soon as the crowd saw him they erupted in a cheer.

"Thank you, thank you, for your Christmas beer!"

THANK YOU, BREWDOLPH!

Brewdolph was happy,

but his work was not yet done.

BEST TOY
EVER
MUST-HAVE TOY

He had to help the world

before Christmas was won.

Brewdolph kicked up, up, up into the air.

He had to visit Santa's helpers while they sat in their chair.

NORTH POLE

He whispered his plan to spread Christmas cheer.

And if you haven't already guessed...

It's all centered around craft beer!

The children told Santa's helpers all that they want.

And Santa's helpers sent the kids on a scavenger hunt.

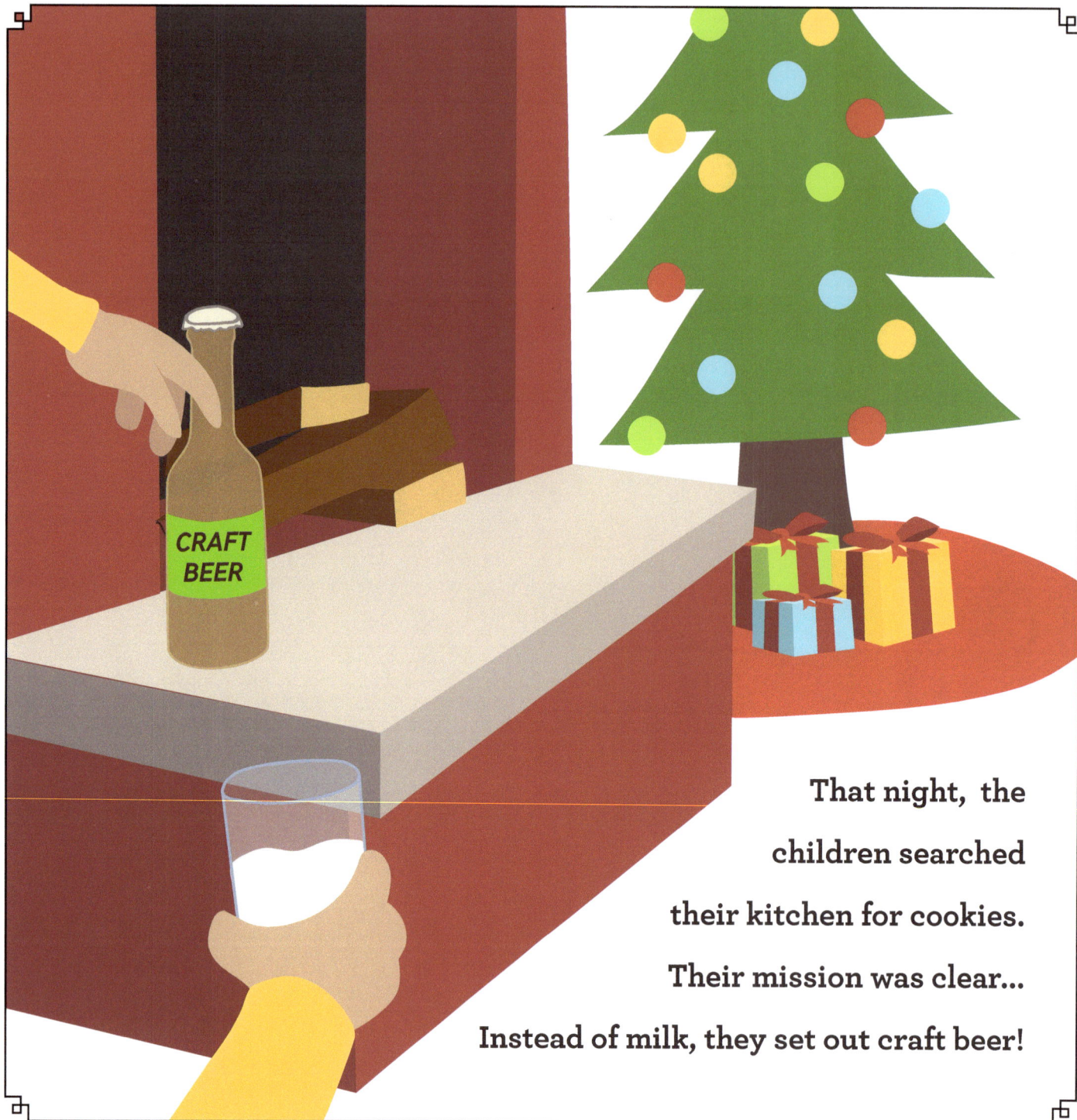

That night, the
children searched
their kitchen for cookies.
Their mission was clear...
Instead of milk, they set out craft beer!

The phones were turned off, and finally, the family got together.

It started to snow, which is perfect Christmas weather.

As the children were put to bed,

it became quite clear.

All night, the parents

had been eyeing the craft beer.

The night grew short and soon all were asleep.

So Santa jumped into the chimney with a leap.

He set out the presents
and collected his gear.

Then he looked and saw;
behold a craft beer!

Santa relaxed and a smile
formed on his jolly face.
It was fine if it took a little longer
and he slowed down his pace.

The next morning the parents were happy.

The children were full of cheer.

Christmas was saved!

Thanks to Brewdolph and his Christmas beer.

Santa and his Reindeer kicked up, up, and away...

He shouted, "To all a good night, and a happy brew day!"

So this year turn off your phones,
and warm your bones.

Join family and friends
within your homes.

CRAFT
BEER

And remember this Christmas season
while you are sitting here,

to have the best Christmas ever,
always give the gift of craft beer.

BrewFund

Give the Gift of Beer

Ready to Give Someone the Gift of a Craft Beer?

With BrewFund you can easily send your friends a craft beer at their favorite breweries and taprooms!

Learn more at: BrewFund.com

Download on the App Store

GET IT ON Google Play

This book was brought to you by the creatives at BrewFund, Inc. Thank you for your support!

Own a brewery? Join BrewFund's free platform!
https://brewfund.com/platform

www.ingramcontent.com/pod-product-compliance
Lightning Source LLC
LaVergne TN
LVHW072055070426
835508LV00002B/110